ANTONIA NOVELLO

U.S. SURGEON GENERAL

JOAN C. HAWXHURST

Consultants:

Dr. Julian Nava
Historian
Former U.S. Ambassador to Mexico

Yolanda Quintanilla-Finley
Teacher and Project Specialist
Corona Unified School District
Corona, California

Hispanic Heritage
The Millbrook Press
Brookfield, Connecticut

Cover photo courtesy of UPI/Bettmann

Photos courtesy of UPI/Bettmann: pp. 3, 14, 16, 17, 18, 29;
Wide World Photos: pp. 4, 23, 24, 25, 27; The Rowland Co.: p.
7; FPG International, © Farrell Grehan: p. 8; The University of
Michigan News and Information Services, photo by Bob Kalmbach:
p. 13; Press Office of Antonia Novello: pp. 20, 22.

Library of Congress Cataloging-in-Publication Data
Hawxhurst, Joan C.
Antonia Novello, U.S. surgeon general / by Joan C. Hawxhurst.
p.   cm.—(Hispanic heritage)
Includes bibliographical references and index.
Summary: A biography of President Bush's Surgeon General, focusing
on her childhood in Puerto Rico, personal medical problems, training
and practice as a pediatrician, and opinions on today's health
issues.
ISBN 1-56294-299-9 (lib. bdg.) ISBN 1-56294-862-8 (pbk.)
1. Novello, Antonia C.—Juvenile literature.   2. Health officers—
United States—Biography—Juvenile literature.   3. Pediatricians—
United States—Biography—Juvenile literature. [1. Novello,
Antonia C.   2. Health officers.   3. Physicians.   4. Puerto Ricans—
Biography.] I. Title. II. Series.
R154.N82H39   1993
610'.92—dc20   [B]   92-19564   CIP   AC

Published by The Millbrook Press
2 Old New Milford Road
Brookfield, Connecticut 06804

ANTONIA NOVELLO

Supreme Court Associate Justice Sandra Day O'Connor swears in the new U.S. Surgeon General, Dr. Antonia Novello, on March 9, 1990. Antonia's mother and husband stand beside her, and President George Bush looks on.

O*n a winter day in 1990,* a small group of people gathered at the White House in Washington, D.C., for a special ceremony. President George Bush stood facing Dr. Antonia Coello Novello. Novello's mother and husband stood by her side. She raised her right hand, and Bush officially made her the fourteenth Surgeon General of the United States.

The Surgeon General is the country's leading health expert. Antonia Novello, at age forty-five, became both the first woman to hold this position and the first Hispanic. She promised to speak for those people "who have never been able to speak for themselves."

During the ceremony, Novello thought back to the place where she had grown up, thousands of miles from the nation's capital. She remembered how as a little girl, nicknamed Tonita, she had dreamed of becoming a doctor. Her dream had come true. In fact, more than she had ever dared to dream was coming true. She felt proud of her Hispanic heritage, and she was determined to be an example for children. She wanted them to believe that if this woman from Puerto Rico could rise so far, then so too could they.

THE GIRL FROM FAJARDO · Antonia Coello, or Tonita, was born on August 23, 1944, on the beautiful island of Puerto Rico, whose sandy beaches were washed by the Atlantic Ocean and the Caribbean Sea. In 1952, Puerto Rico became a special part of the United States called a commonwealth. This means that although Puerto Rico was not one of the fifty states, its three million inhabitants were American citizens.

Puerto Rico has a long history of European settlement—in fact, longer than any other part of the United States. The Spanish began settling the island in 1508, about a century before the British began to live in North America. The island's first inhabitants were Arawaks. About fifty years after the arrival of the Spanish, almost the entire Arawak population had been wiped out.

Puerto Rico, which means "rich port" in Spanish, remains mostly a Spanish culture. Its citizens speak Spanish, and there are many beautiful Spanish-style churches and public buildings surrounded by palm trees and brightly colored tropical flowers. Most people are Catholics, and they observe Spanish traditions and customs. But because Puerto Rico is part of the United States,

Many of San Juan's buildings, such as this centuries-old Cristo Chapel, date back to the time when the Spanish ruled Puerto Rico.

U.S. mainland ways have blended into the culture. Many U.S. products are sold there, and the government is modeled on that of the United States.

Tonita first lived in a public housing project in Fajardo, a small town on the eastern end of the island. Her family soon moved to a small house in the center of town. Most of the townspeople worked on nearby farms. They were too poor to eat well or to pay for expensive doctors, so many of the children were in bad health.

Point Sardina on the north-eastern shore of Puerto Rico.

Tonita's parents, Antonio and Ana Delia Flores Coello, did not have much money either. There was little to spend on fancy clothes and toys. But Tonita was an active child who wore jeans most of the time anyway. She loved playing with her brother, Thomas, and their dog and horse.

When Tonita was very young, her parents divorced, and by the time she was four years old, her father had died. Her mother remarried. Tonita liked her stepfather.

Tonita's mother was a teacher, and eventually she became a principal at Yabucoa High School. Because the school was far away, her mother had to spend most nights there during the week. Even though she was usually only home on the weekends, Tonita's mother was very close to her children.

Ana Delia taught her children to work hard in school. She told them that school would help them have a better life. The Coello children were taught to care about other people and to respect them.

Even though Tonita had fun as a girl, going to the movies on Saturday afternoons and playing softball with her many friends at a nearby park, she was sick much of the time. She had been born with a problem in her colon that made her weak and tired. (The colon is part of the large intestine, which helps digest food after it passes through the stomach.) Sometimes Tonita's colon would swell up, making her very uncomfortable. Every summer she had to spend several weeks in the hospital. There, her disease was treated, and the swelling would go down.

The doctors played games with Tonita, and they were gentle when they gave her shots. But even though they made her feel better, the truth was that only a surgeon, a specially trained doctor, could really help Tonita get well. What she needed was an operation. But the hospital was in a distant town. Since Tonita's mother had to work, she could not take the long trip. So for years Tonita did not have the operation.

In the meantime, Tonita decided that she would become a doctor. She did not want other children to have to wait for their operations the way she had to. And she wanted to care for the many sick children in Fajardo.

She knew that she would have to study very hard to turn her dream into a reality. Tonita studied Spanish and English, and she did her homework every day. Besides getting very good grades in school, she became a Girl Scout and continued to play softball. She also acted in school plays and sang in the high school chorus.

By the end of high school, all of Tonita's hard work began to bring her rewards. She was chosen to speak at her high school graduation in 1961. The people of Fajardo also honored her by picking her to be the queen of a very special town celebration called the Patron Saint Festival.

ANTONIA, MEDICAL STUDENT · When Tonita was eighteen, she told her mother that she wanted to have the operation to fix her colon. Her mother agreed, and Tonita went to the special hospital. The operation was not completely successful, but Tonita felt much better.

By this time, people started calling Tonita by her real name—Antonia. She still dreamed of being a doctor. Because she earned very good grades in high school, Antonia received a scholarship, money to pay for her schooling. Antonia went to the University of Puerto Rico in Rio Piedras. There, she studied biology, the science that deals with living things.

When she was almost finished with college, Antonia applied to medical schools. She knew that only the best students were accepted, so she waited nervously for a reply. She only told her mother that she had applied after the University of Puerto Rico had accepted her. She had been too afraid to disappoint her if she hadn't gotten in. Her mother was thrilled. She told Antonia that if she worked hard, she could do anything she wanted.

In the fall of 1965, Antonia began her medical training in San Juan, the capital city of Puerto Rico. During her first year there, Antonia faced two hardships. First, her favorite aunt died because of a problem with her kidneys. The doctors had not known how to fix them. Antonia then decided to become a kidney specialist. She promised herself that when she was a doctor, no one in her family would die because a doctor did not know what to do.

The second challenge that Antonia faced was related to the problem with her colon. She got very sick and had to have a second operation. This time, her doctors sent her to a hospital in Minnesota. Antonia was twenty years old at the time. She was afraid to travel thousands of miles from Puerto Rico by herself. But she knew that she had to.

The surgery was very successful. After her body started to heal, she went back to medical school. But for a while, her colon leaked. She had to wear diapers for six months! She later said, "I have survived many times in my life by learning to laugh at myself—that's the best medicine. But I also became very self-assured and capable of saying that if I could do that [wear diapers], I could do anything!"

While she was in medical school, Antonia met Joseph Novello, a doctor who worked for the United States Navy near Fajardo. Antonia and Joseph fell in love, and the day after Antonia graduated from medical school in 1970, they got married.

Antonia and her new husband moved to Ann Arbor, Michigan. There, Antonia worked as an intern at the University of Michigan. This was the final step before becoming a doctor.

The University of Michigan hospital, where Antonia worked as an intern after graduating from medical school.

In the mornings, before she went to the hospital, Antonia often went to a nearby pond. She would watch the ducks and think about things. She had not forgotten her dream of taking care of the children of her hometown. Novello decided to become a pediatrician, a specialist in children's health.

The doctors at the University of Michigan saw that Antonia was very talented. They named her Intern of the Year. This was the first time that a woman had received the award.

DOCTOR ANTONIA NOVELLO · Now Antonia was called Dr. Antonia Novello. In the 1970s there weren't many women doctors. People often thought that Dr. Novello was a nurse. She had to explain over and over that she was a doctor.

In the 1970s, when Antonia Novello began to practice medicine, women doctors were rare.

Dr. Novello and her husband lived in Michigan for five years, where Antonia learned all about sick children. Finally, when she was ready to open her own office, she and her husband moved to Washington, D.C.

In Washington, Dr. Antonia Novello cared for babies and young children. Many of them did not get enough to eat or had come down with a terrible sickness. Sometimes when Novello was talking to the parents about their children's condition, she became so sad that she would cry.

After two years, Dr. Novello decided to give up her practice. She later said, "When the pediatrician cries as much as the parents do, then you know it's time to get out."

Novello went to work for the U.S. Public Health Service instead. This government organization teaches people how to stay healthy by providing information about good health habits and disease. Novello was happier in her new job, which was devoted to helping children and adults to *not* get sick.

For a year, Dr. Novello helped write laws about health issues. These included a law about giving body organs such as hearts and kidneys to people who needed them. Another law required cigarette manufacturers to put warnings about the dangers of smoking on their packaging.

SMOKE FREE CLASS OF 2000

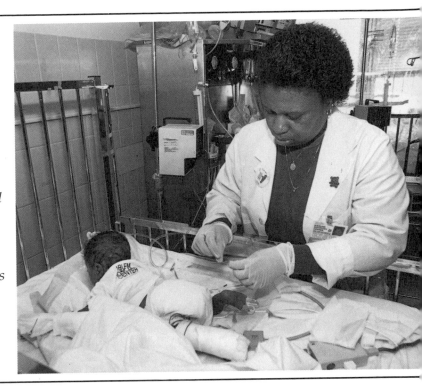

Left: As a member of the U.S. Public Health Service, Novello was active in promoting good health among children. She was especially concerned with the dangers of smoking.

Right: This baby has been infected with the AIDS virus.

In Washington, Dr. Novello began to see children who had been infected with the virus that causes AIDS, a deadly disease with no known cure. AIDS was first identified in the early 1980s and is now one of the gravest health problems facing the nation—and the world—today.

Dr. Novello thought that there should be more government money set aside for researching a cure for AIDS. She presented a government report showing that AIDS

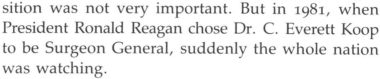

SURGEON GENERAL
C. EVERETT KOOP

The main job of the Surgeon General is to help shape our country's policies on health-related issues such as smoking, AIDS, alcohol and drugs, and nutrition. In the past, this po-

sition was not very important. But in 1981, when President Ronald Reagan chose Dr. C. Everett Koop to be Surgeon General, suddenly the whole nation was watching.

Everyone knew that Koop was very conservative. They were sure that he would use his office to make his own feelings public. He surprised people, though. He did not do that.

For example, Koop believed very strongly that it was wrong for people to have sex when they weren't married. But because of the great danger of young people getting AIDS, he encouraged schools to give classes on sex education. Koop also led a very strong campaign against smoking.

Reagan, the Republican party, and many businesspeople (especially the ones who ran tobacco companies) were angry that Koop refused to support their position. But Koop felt that even if he agreed with the Republicans, the country needed a doctor who was not tempted to push his or her private or political views on the public. C. Everett Koop, like Antonia Novello, saw himself as a doctor, not a politician.

was the number nine cause of death among children from one to four years old. (Some children get AIDS if they are born to mothers who have the virus.) Novello also warned that the number of teenagers infected with AIDS was probably much greater than people realized.

President George Bush was so pleased with Novello's work that, in 1989, he offered her the job of Surgeon General of the United States. She was so excited that she screamed out loud: "I'm *patidifusa!*" ("overwhelmed").

People wondered what Dr. Antonia Novello would be like as the new Surgeon General. Would she be as outspoken as Dr. C. Everett Koop, the man who held the position before her? One thing was certain, though. Hispanic people were proud that a Puerto Rican had been chosen for such a high office. And women were proud of her, too.

But before she could show the world what she would do as Surgeon General, the U.S. Senate had to vote on whether or not she should get the job.

SURGEON GENERAL NOVELLO · The Senate voted her in and on March 9, 1990, she was sworn in as Surgeon General. Dr. Novello became one of the most famous doctors in the United States. It seemed as if everyone wanted to know her opinions about important health matters. For her first public appearance as Surgeon General, Novello decided to return to Puerto Rico.

*Antonia Novello was thrilled to be sworn in as
the Surgeon General of the United States.*

In Fajardo, four thousand people came to see her. They gathered in the park where she had played softball as a little girl. She greeted her friends and neighbors with a kiss on the cheek. As she walked along the streets, people stopped to talk to her. Many women hugged her. Dr. Novello said, "They looked at me [as proof] that their grandchildren could grow up to be Surgeon General, to be in an important position. I realized . . . I have to be good as a woman, I have to be good as a Hispanic."

Dr. Novello knew that she faced many challenges ahead. She would have to be a strong and wise health leader to help the nation face such serious problems as AIDS. Dr. Novello went back to Washington to start her new job.

TAKING CARE OF AMERICA · As Surgeon General, Antonia Novello took charge of the U.S. Public Health Service. She wore a dark blue uniform with brass buttons and five rows of colored medals. With her staff, Dr. Novello began to collect information about the common health problems of Americans. She said that her motto— her favorite description of good health—was "good science and good sense." By "good science," she meant that it was important to learn as much as possible about disease. "Good sense" meant that people needed to think about what they were doing—and be careful.

Novello spent a lot of time visiting classrooms and talking to schoolchildren about health issues.

Dr. Novello wanted to see better health care for many different groups of Americans. She said: "I hope that being the first woman and minority Surgeon General . . . enables me to reach many individuals with my message of empowerment [greater power] for women, children, and minorities."

Novello's love of children did not lessen when she became the nation's official doctor. She decorated the waiting room of her new office with objects that she treasured: dolls and children's artwork. She filled her office with teddy bears. She put an unopened bottle of wine on her desk as a reminder of the need to keep children from using alcohol.

Part of her job involved studying AIDS. She visited mothers who had the disease. She also played with small children infected with the AIDS virus.

Novello reads to a three-year-old girl with AIDS before speaking at a luncheon to kick off a support program for families with AIDS.

Novello holds a six-pack of alcohol during a Washington, D.C., news conference in November 1991 and criticizes the advertising directed at young people.

In a special report, Dr. Novello said that by the end of 1990 almost three thousand children under thirteen years of age had been reported as having AIDS. She said that many more such cases had not been reported. Most of these children were born with the AIDS virus because their mothers had the virus. Dr. Novello warned that many children would lose their parents because of the disease.

Novello also began to explore the effects of alcohol, another major health problem affecting children. In 1991 she reported that "more than half of all junior and senior high-school students drink alcohol and almost half a million go on a drinking spree every week."

"Alcohol remains the number one drug problem among our youth," said Dr. Novello. Drunk driving "remains one of the leading causes of death among our youth. Yet kids still think drinking is cool."

Each year Novello has released a report on the dangers of smoking cigarettes. She says it is never too late to quit and save one's health.

Cigarette smoking was also an issue that Dr. Novello took on. She expressed her worry that more and more women were smoking. Lung cancer, which can be caused by smoking, had become the leading cause of cancer death among women. Novello said that people needed to know that smoking tobacco led to 390,000 deaths every year in the United States. She wanted insurance companies to help pay for programs to help people stop smoking.

The Surgeon General was also aware of the unique health concerns of people in minority groups. She recently helped write a report showing that many Hispanic Americans were not getting the medical care and health insurance that they needed. She found that many Hispanic-American women and children were getting AIDS, and many Hispanics were dying of cancer and suffering from problems with drugs and violence.

Dr. Novello spoke out against some advertisements on television and in magazines. Many of these ads were trying to get young people to smoke cigarettes or drink alcohol. Dr. Novello worked very hard to put a stop to these ads.

"I want all Americans to be healthy and safe," she said, "to have the best out of life and to bring the best to life."

THE BEST OF LIFE · Even with the many demands Antonia Novello faced as the new Surgeon General, she never forgot that there was more to life than hard work. She continued to believe in regular exercise to relax and stay healthy. Every day she walked with her husband around their neighborhood of Georgetown in Washington, D.C., and three times a week she exercised with people from her office. Listening to classical music and

HISPANIC-AMERICAN HEALTH

One problem Surgeon General Novello is trying to solve is the poor health of many Hispanic Americans. Dr. Novello led a team of experts to gather health and medical information about Hispanic Americans. Here is what they found:

- More Hispanic Americans have kidney disease than do other Americans.

- Fewer Hispanic Americans get shots to prevent measles.

- The number of deaths from some kinds of cancer is higher for Hispanic Americans.

- Hispanic-American women and children are being especially hard hit by AIDS.

The parents of this family have AIDS and are worried about who will take care of their children. Novello cares very much about helping people like this.

Dr. Novello points out that Hispanic Americans are made up of many different groups. Millions are Mexican Americans. Many others are Cuban Americans and Puerto Ricans. Still others are from families that came from other Spanish-speaking areas. Not all Hispanic Americans suffer equally from these problems.

watching movies were other ways she liked to relax— and have fun.

Dr. Novello and her husband did not have children of their own. But in a sense, from the time she became Surgeon General, Novello considered all children to be her special concern. And then, she would never travel far without her cat, Nicolosa.

Antonia Novello became a model for others, especially Hispanics and women. She said that the story of her life showed that people could do anything. A poor girl from the town of Fajardo, Puerto Rico, Novello rose to hold the post of Surgeon General of the United States. If she could do that, she said, anyone could do anything. It just took hard work and a dream.

Many children from around the country wrote letters to Dr. Novello. One of her favorite ones was written by a nine-year-old girl. It said, "I'm intelligent and I want to be the second woman Surgeon General."

When Antonia Novello had realized her dream of becoming a doctor, she did not stop. She went on to become the leading doctor of the United States. And even then, she continued to dream. She wanted children to look at her and know that, if they decided to, they could become Surgeon General, too. Or they could be whatever they wanted to be.

In her March 1992 address at an anti-smoking
conference, Dr. Novello warned: " . . . if current trends
continue, ten years from now we will be witnessing the
presence of yet another addicted generation."

IMPORTANT EVENTS IN
THE LIFE OF ANTONIA NOVELLO

1944	Antonia Coello is born on August 23 in Fajardo, Puerto Rico.
1961	Antonia graduates from high school.
1962	Antonia has an operation on her colon.
1965	Antonia graduates from college at the University of Puerto Rico's Rio Piedras campus with a bachelor of science degree.
1970	Antonia earns her medical degree from the University of Puerto Rico in San Juan. She and Dr. Joseph Novello marry.
1970–1973	Dr. Antonia Novello works as an intern and then a resident at the University of Michigan Medical Center in Ann Arbor.
1974–1975	Novello works as an expert in children's kidney diseases at Georgetown University Hospital in Washington, D.C.
1976–1978	Novello runs her own private medical practice in Washington, D.C.
1978–1990	Novello works at the U.S. Public Health Service.
1990	Dr. Antonia Novello becomes the Surgeon General of the United States.

FIND OUT MORE ABOUT HEALTH ISSUES
THAT CONCERN DR. ANTONIA NOVELLO

Crack and Cocaine by Marcy C. Turck. New York: Macmillan, 1990.

Facts About Alcohol by Jeffrey Gunn. Baxter, Minn.: Knowledge Publications, 1990.

Understanding and Preventing AIDS: A Guide for Young People by Warren Coleman. Chicago, Ill.: Childrens Press, 1988.

Why Do People Smoke? by Pete Sanders. New York: Franklin Watts, 1989.

FIND OUT MORE
ABOUT PUERTO RICO

Puerto Rico in Pictures edited by the Department of Geography Staff of Lerner Publications. Minneapolis, Minn.: Lerner, 1987.

Take a Trip to Puerto Rico by John Griffiths. New York: Franklin Watts, 1989.

INDEX

Page numbers in *italics* refer to illustrations.